Renshi

Roseann O'Reilly Runte

RENSHI

Poetry

University of Ottawa Press
2026

Les **Presses** de l'Université d'Ottawa
University of Ottawa **Press**

Les Presses de l'Université d'Ottawa / University of Ottawa Press (PUO-UOP) is North America's flagship bilingual university press, affiliated to one of Canada's top research universities. PUO-UOP enriches the intellectual and cultural discourse of our increasingly knowledge-based and globalized world with peer-reviewed, award-winning books.

www.Press.uOttawa.ca

Library and Archives Canada Cataloguing in Publication

Title: Renshi / Roseann O'Reilly Runte.
Names: O'Reilly Runte, Roseann, author.
Description: Series statement: Essays and fictions | Text chiefly in English; poem in English, French, Korean and Japanese.
Identifiers: Canadiana (print) 20260206040 | Canadiana (ebook) 20260206814 | ISBN 9782760347571 (softcover) | ISBN 9782760347588 (EPUB) | ISBN 9782760347595 (PDF)
Subjects: LCSH: Renga. | LCSH: Renga—Authorship. | LCGFT: Essays. | LCGFT: Renga.
Classification: LCC PN6110.R42 O74 2026 | DDC 808.81/4—dc23

Legal Deposit: Third Quarter 2026
Library and Archives Canada

Production Team

Copy-editing	Seunghee Chung, Tanina Drvar, Annie Pronovost, Mami Sasaki, Hyounjeong Yoo
Proofreading	Julie Boissonneault, Seunghee Chung, Céline Parent, Mami Sasaki, Yoriko Aizu
Typesetting	Ediscript enr.
Cover design	Dany Lagueux

Cover Image

Sylviane de Roquebrune, 1992

uOttawa

PUO-UOP gratefully acknowledges the funding support of the University of Ottawa, the Government of Canada, the Canada Council for the Arts, the Ontario Arts Council and the Government of Ontario.

Canada | Canada Council for the Arts | Conseil des arts du Canada | Ontario Arts Council | Conseil des arts de l'Ontario | Ontario

Poetry by
Makoto Ooka
Shuntaro Tanikawa
Yong-Jik Kim
Roseann O'Reilly Runte

Foreword by
Ted Goossen

Cover Art by
Sylviane de Roquebrune

Table of Contents

Dedication

In these chaotic times when our planet is buffeted by storms and droughts, raging fires, hunger, violence, and sadness, we more than ever need the inspiration and beauty of poetry. We invite you to take a few moments to reflect on a unique international dialogue. Collaboration across continents, oceans, and time zones has the potential to inspire our creative spirits and collective wisdom, enabling a renaissance of fresh ideas.

It is in this spirit that we present this linked poem written simultaneously in four languages over two days, during which the world celebrated the sporting prowess and energy of youth at a major competition in Tokyo. At the same time, we witnessed news clips of an uprising in the Soviet legislature that would mark the beginning of the dissolution of the Soviet empire of the day and the end of the Cold War.

The renowned Japanese poets Makoto Ooka and Shuntaro Tanikawa were at the heart of this collaboration and were joined by celebrated Korean poet Yong-Jik Kim and Canadian poet Roseann O'Reilly Runte. We entered into a unique exercise in sharing culture and language, philosophical thought, and traditional artistic forms. The result was a poem with twenty-four verses, each responding to the one before and together forming a meaningful whole. It was 1991 and we dared to hope. We offer this work now in memory of those who are no longer with us, but who have left this poetic legacy, which provides, yet today, reason to hope.

This work is now being presented in print for the first time and is shared with you in the memory of Makoto Ooka, Shuntaro Tanikawa, and Yong-Jik Kim who are no longer with us and whom we recognize with gratitude. They continue to inspire their readers by daring us to follow them in transcending international boundaries and the linguistic and cultural blinkers we all wear. There could not be a more fitting memorial for these extraordinary poets and a more appropriate time to nurture the seeds of global dialogue that they planted.

In Memoriam

This work is dedicated to the late Professor Toru Haga, to poets Makoto Ooka, Shuntaro Tanikawa, and Yong-Jik Kim, and violinist Oliver Schroer.

This project would never have been imagined without the creative and compelling vision and energy of Dr. Toru Haga. He decided to bring together the worlds of literary creation and literary criticism by creating an international, multilingual event that demonstrated and encouraged writers and critics the world over to share inspiration and understanding in an era and world where so much was possible but where we often failed to perceive and pursue noble goals. Dr. Toru Haga not only had an extraordinary concept in mind, but he also had the persuasive power of his own eloquence and the respect of his country to enable this significant project.

Makoto Ooka, one of the leading Japanese poets of this century, was also an expert scholar and mass communicator, writing poetry and explaining the meaning of verses that were part of Japanese traditions. His poetry appeared daily on the front page of a major Japanese newspaper and in the dozens of volumes of his beautiful verses, which received international recognition and the highest honours in Japan. He led the group of poets involved in this project, patiently explaining the traditions and rules to the international poets and adapting the form to the circumstances, as this was the first time a *renshi* had been composed in four languages at once.

Shuntaro Tanikawa was a brilliant poet whose creative work embraced many forms, including film and music, animation, and traditional verse. Born in the same year as Ooka, their strong friendship and understanding served to inspire the writers of this *renshi*. Tanikawa was known for his extraordinary work, which was internationally applauded and had received the highest honours. He was patient and his kindly sense of humour was much appreciated throughout this poetic adventure.

Yong-Jik Kim was a celebrated poet, translator, and professor at the Seoul National University. Member of the Republic of Korea's National Academy of the Arts, his poetry and scholarly works were awarded the Modern Literature Prize, the Sejong Culture Prize, and the Republic of Korea Literature Prize, among others. He was president of the Korean Society for Poetics, the Korean Comparative Literature Society, and the Literary Translation Institute of Korea.

Oliver Schroer, a talented Canadian violinist and composer, was well known in Europe and the United States. During his short lifetime, he recorded over one hundred albums and graciously embraced this project, joining the group of musicians who came together in Canada to create and perform their composition that would accompany the poem.

Setting the Stage

Toru Haga, at that time a distinguished professor of literature at the International Research Center for Japanese Studies in Kyoto, was also president of the International Comparative Literature Association, which included several thousand scholars from around the world who came together for a major conference every three years. Haga was thus responsible for the conference that was held in Tokyo in August 1991.

He wished to take that opportunity to break through the boundaries between literature and criticism and embarked on an innovative project. Thinking that literary critics and scholars and the creative writers themselves would benefit from having a better understanding of the process of creation, on the one hand, and the discipline of criticism on the other, he devised a plan to bring together poets and critics. He invited four poets to assemble during the conference to create a linked poem in situ and in real time. They were instructed to follow the structure and rules that had been laid out centuries ago when Japanese poets would come together at a castle to write a *renga*, which would be presented in public the following day. However, in Tokyo of 1991, the poets would present their work to the scholars who were attending the conference along with their guests. By inviting four poets from around the world, Haga modernized the medieval concept by internationalizing the experience. Requesting that the poem be composed simultaneously in four languages, he raised the level of the challenge. This had never been done previously, nor since, to our knowledge. One poet would draft a verse and as soon as it was completed, they would explain it to the next poet, who began to compose the verse that would follow in response while a more polished translation was being committed to paper. Thus, when the poem was complete, it existed as a whole in each of the four languages: Japanese, Korean, English, and French. The soundtrack at the conclusion of this volume, for which there is a link, includes a live recording of the event, when the poets emerged breathlessly from the room where they had been working to meet the public assembled. Both the English and the French versions were written by Roseann Runte, the Korean by Yong-Jik Kim, and the Japanese alternately by Makoto Ooka and Shuntaro Tanikawa.

When the poets returned to their homes after the conference, they were followed by a great wave of enthusiasm and repeated requests for another public reading. Roseann Runte decided to embellish the theme of uniting creative approaches by including music, dance, art, and poetry. She invited artist Sylviane de Roquebrune to illustrate the verses and musicians Casey Sokol, David Mott, Oliver Schroer, and Richard "Dick" Armin to compose music to accompany our words. The Japan Foundation in Toronto arranged for the Butoh dance group Uno Man to choreograph a dance to the music. This was then performed in Toronto on October 10, 1992. You will also find, at the end of this publication, a link to a sample of an improvisational composition by Casey Sokol, which is a fitting reminiscence of the event.

Following this multidisciplinary performance, the poets, musicians, artists, and dancers all turned to their next commitments and continued their busy lives. However, they all asked Roseann Runte to see that this international, multilingual, and now interdisciplinary work was preserved and made widely available. Subsequently the proceedings of the scholarly presentations at the conference were published in six volumes under the direction of Haga and Earl Miner. Roseann Runte was responsible for the second volume,

Visions of Beauty, which she edited with Hans R. Runte and which was published by the University of Tokyo Press in 1995. The *renshi* project awaited Roseann's attention while she dedicated her time to her career in academic leadership.

Time passed but the project was never forgotten. It was a singular performance of creative genius and inspiration for the poets, artists, musicians, and all in attendance. It also referred to an important moment in history. *Renga* and *renshi* poems must, according to custom, include a reference to what is happening at the time of writing. That August day in 1991, when the *renshi* was composed, the poets listened carefully to the news. It was the very day the Soviet Parliament was stormed, marking the rapid end of the Cold War. The poem speaks to the power of poetry and philosophy and the necessity for international dialogue in the face of oppression. It expresses the belief that the words of the poets will outlive violence and bring hope to future generations.

Despite the passage of time and career demands, Runte wished to keep her word to see that this work might become available to inspire readers and poets, artists, and musicians around the world. She wanted to commemorate this important artistic event and pay tribute to Haga and her fellow poets and artists, who have since passed away.

Today, more than ever, the world needs thoughtful dialogue that will bridge oceans and cross continents. It is high time for words of wisdom and peace and the saving grace and beauty of poetry.

Foreword

By Ted Goossen

The following linked poem, composed by four poets from three countries during a two-day period in August 1991, is the modern expression of an old literary form—the Japanese *renga* or *renku*—which has been around for over seven hundred years, and which ranked with the thirty-one-syllable *waka* as the dominant poetic form in Japan from the fifteenth to the eighteenth century. Yet how surprised Basho, one of the great masters of the genre, would be to see what new branches have been grafted on that ancient trunk, and what rare flowers now bloom there! We present some of them here—twenty-four stanzas in four languages—so that you too may enjoy their fragrance and perhaps be enticed to think about poetry and its creation in fresh and challenging ways. First, though, let us give you a peek at how this experiment in linked poetry transpired, and how it is connected to the old tradition.

August in Tokyo is normally a sticky, sweltering month, hardly conducive, one would think, to any endeavour, poetic or otherwise. Neither would one expect an international academic conference—in this case that of the International Comparative Literature Association (ICLA)—to provide a promising venue for a poetic gathering, critics and scholars being a notoriously difficult, even antagonistic audience. Yet the weather was surprisingly pleasant, and the large, air-conditioned room where the poem came into being, perched on the tenth floor of one of Aoyama Gakuin University's most modern buildings, was a perfect refuge, a sealed world set apart from the hustle and bustle of the ongoing conference. There we lived for two days, eating and working together, a small colony of translators, support staff, and the four poets themselves: Yong-Jik Kim of South Korea, Roseann O'Reilly Runte of Canada, and Shuntaro Tanikawa and Makoto Ooka of Japan. Ooka was very much the centre of the group, not just because of his abundant charm and energy, but because he himself had pioneered the whole genre of linked free verse, or *renshi,* as he has christened it in Japanese.

Renga, renku, renshi… what do these distressingly similar-looking Japanese terms mean, and how are they related to the linked poem we offer here? *Renga* is the oldest—we might say it is the father to the *renku*, grandfather to the *renshi*. It was practised by groups of poets as early as the thirteenth century, usually as a way of relaxing after an arduous day spent composing *waka*, the most basic and tradition-bound form of Japanese verse. By breaking up the thirty-one-syllable *waka* into seventeen- and fourteen-syllable stanzas, these poets amused themselves by "capping" each other's verses, each trying to maintain some continuity with their predecessor's effort while simultaneously adding an unexpected twist to its implications. *Renga* sessions generally lasted between two and four hours and produced a predetermined number of stanzas. A given stanza was to be read in conjunction with its predecessor or its successor (or by itself), but it was not supposed to be overtly linked to other parts of the poem. Enjoyment was the key to these early *renga* parties, and before long, a number of famous *renga* masters had emerged. They travelled about the countryside, teaching the finer points of the genre to all and sundry.

By the fifteenth century, the *renga* had become the most influential poetic form in Japan. This pre-eminence, however, led to ever further codification. In a standard one-hundred-stanza *renga*, for example, cherry blossoms had to be mentioned four times, the moon seven, always at specified intervals. Whole categories of words were deemed inappropriate, while others—like "dream"—could only be used sparingly, and with certain fixed implications. By the seventeenth century, members of the new *haikai* movement were reacting against this restrictive format, changing it to fit the new demands of the developing Edo culture. The length was reduced to thirty-six stanzas. New topics and diction, which reflected the realities of daily life, were introduced, and much of the humour and spontaneity was restored. The new genre—the "comic" *renga*, later renamed the *renku*—was taken to its highest level by Basho, whom we usually associate with the seventeen-syllable *haiku*, but who, during his lifetime, was better known as the greatest of the comic *renga* masters.

By the late eighteenth century, however, the golden age of linked verse had come to an end. Its last great practitioner, Buson, was more adept at creating great stanzas than great sequences, and by his death, the *haiku*, originally just the opening stanza for the longer *renku*, had eclipsed its aging progenitor. In retrospect, however, it seems somehow remarkable that poetic forms which involved not a single creator, but a small group of like-minded poets, could have stood at the centre of the Japanese literary scene for three centuries. What explains the success of collective authorship in Japan? Is it due to some peculiarly Japanese penchant for group activity, the corollary to the idea that the Japanese are somehow culturally inhibited from succeeding in any truly individual creativity?

Books have been written on this subject, of course, and countless more will follow. Rather than indulge in abstract speculation, let us return to that sprawling, air-conditioned room with its small community of poets and translators, for it is there that some concrete answers may be found. It is the morning of the first day and Ooka has given general instructions—alternating stanzas of five and three lines in free-verse form, attention paid to specific season and place, no repeated images, save the most powerful stanzas for the end—and he set Tanikawa to produce the first verse. Tanikawa scribbles and erases, scribbles and erases. Finally, he is ready. Ooka takes a look. No, he says, this is not quite right. For a second, the tension in the room increases, the non-Japanese poets in particular cringing at the prospect of having their own work similarly disparaged. Yet Tanikawa seems not the least bit flustered. Calmly and cheerfully, he plunges back into his creation, making a change here, an edit there. This time Ooka is satisfied, and the ball is passed to the Canadian, Roseann O'Reilly Runte. But before she can begin, she must see the translated version of Tanikawa's poem. With Tanikawa looking over one shoulder and Runte over the other, the translator suddenly finds herself in a new and unfamiliar situation. Translating poetry is a highly problematic (some would say impossible) task at the best of times, but under these conditions... Yet, here too, the poets are helpful and supportive; allies instead of opponents, they pitch in to get the translation to the point where Runte can begin her three-line stanza. The *renshi* composition is now fully under way.

Ooka's concept of *renshi* is far more liberal than anything even Basho could ever have envisaged. Syllable count is irrelevant; there are no required (or proscribed) words or topics, and other limitations on poetic diction are clearly unworkable given the vagaries of poetic translation. Yet some central elements seem to have been retained. Except for the first and last stanza in the cycle, each stanza has three distinct "identities," as a composite poem in tandem with either the stanza preceding or following it, and as an independent verse in its own right. Ooka's role as teacher and critic likewise mirrors that of the old masters. He commands an overview of the total work, and his criticisms, even when harsh (one stanza is rejected for having "adhered" too closely to the one preceding it), are taken in the generous spirit with which they were intended. Gradually, that naked, exposed feeling, which had initially terrified poets and translators alike, is replaced by a sense of solidarity and commitment to a common goal. As the hours pass, and meals, wine, and laughter are shared, the atmosphere grows more friendly and relaxed, so relaxed in fact that composing more poems after dinner was clearly out of the question.

We find ourselves paying for that party on the second and final day. We are expected to present our completed *renshi* to a large audience in mid-afternoon, but by late morning it is obvious that we will have to lower our sights from the planned thirty-six to a more manageable twenty-four. Even so, the last few hours are hectic, with translators scrambling to keep up with the poets' steady flow of new verse. Poems and translations are under constant discussion—in fact, all the usual boundaries dividing the creation, criticism, and translation of literature seem to have disappeared completely. All we care about is somehow bringing this, our joint creation, to a successful conclusion.

When we stagger down to face the waiting throng, the twenty-third stanza is being translated, and the twenty-fourth is in the process of being composed. We are nearly an hour late, but the audience does not seem to mind. Perhaps they are amused by our excited, somewhat dishevelled appearances! Led by conference organizer, Professor Haga, who scheduled the event in the belief that it would display the creative side of "comparative" literature, the large paper scroll of poems is unfurled and taped against the wall behind us. Copied in Ooka's deft brush strokes, it lends an appropriately traditional aesthetic touch to the proceedings. After Ooka introduces the crowd to the basics of *renshi* composition, each poet describes what went into the making of several of his or her stanzas, a rare glimpse into the creative process that fascinates not just the audience, but the other members of the group as well. Then the linked poem is recited in all four languages, the audience departs, and we are left to bid each other fond adieux, tired yet exhilarated by our shared experience, and perhaps a bit reluctant to see it come to an end.

In a sense, however, I doubt that it has truly ended. Certainly, the act of composing and translating poetry within such a varied and international group leaves a lasting imprint, not just because of the human ties that result, but because it subtly affects our understanding of the creative process itself. As Ooka has pointed out, the "solitary heart" of the poet finds new energy when it reaches out to participate artistically and socially in the "banquet" of shared creation. Contrary to what one might think, "individuality" is not lost in this process; instead, it is paradoxically provided with a warm, congenial space in which to spread its wings. As Tanikawa's verse, the sixteenth in our poem suggests, there is really no question of merging with the group. In poetry as in pickles, we all have our inevitable likes and dislikes. By understanding and playing off these personal and cultural differences, however, it is possible to incorporate new perspectives and expand our own experience of art and life. If some of that feeling comes across to you when you read this embodiment of our efforts, we are satisfied. And if there are those among you who are curious, and who are tempted to try composing linked verse yourselves, let us offer you a final word of encouragement—you do not have to be Japanese to enjoy *renshi*!

The Creation of the Text

It was one of those brilliantly sunny days when all seemed right with the world. A letter from Japan arrived on my desk and things got even better. The International Comparative Literature Association (ICLA) was to meet in Tokyo in August 1991, and the envelope contained a special invitation from distinguished Dr. Toru Haga, who was president of the ICLA and convener of the conference. Interested in the ways creative writing and literary criticism were interrelated, he wanted to encourage a conversation between poets and scholars (creators and critics) during the conference in Tokyo. He proposed a truly global dialogue that would push literary scholarship in a new direction and restore an element of creativity to its critical dimension. At the same time, he sought a new vision for communication in which voices from around the world would compose an inclusive work of art. He was inviting me to join in a collaborative writing project during the conference, the results of which would be presented to the critics, scholars, and media present. Today, as this project is being shared and its spot in history preserved, it is fitting to pay homage to Haga, whom we will remember with the greatest respect for his life's work and for the privilege of his friendship.

I was overjoyed and could hardly believe the honour of receiving this extraordinary invitation. While the Académie française had awarded me the Coppée Prize for poetry, I was principally known in Canada as an academic and head of a college. Writing was the occupation of my solitary hours. To be invited to collaborate with other poets was like offering water to someone crossing the desert. The following day, I floated as if on a cloud and posted my letter of acceptance.

The next letter I received indicated that Makoto Ooka and Shuntaro Tanikawa had also accepted the invitation, and we would be writing a *renga* or *renshi*, the term coined by Makoto Ooka who was a university professor at the Tokyo National University of Fine Arts and Music, director of the Japan Artists Association, chairman of the Japan Contemporary Poetry Society, and chair of the Japan P.E.N. Club. He had written many volumes of poetry and had pioneered a linked poetry collaborative, which included poets from around the world who would spend several days together to write *renshi*. As if this were not sufficient, seven days a week for more than twenty years, a poem written or explained by Ooka had appeared on the front page of the *Asahi Shimbun*, Japan's leading national newspaper. Ooka was an extraordinary poet, highly educated and extremely prolific. Noting the presence of a poem in an important Japanese daily paper, I imagined, for all of two seconds, a similar occurrence in North America. Would *The Globe and Mail* or *The New York Times* consider publishing a poem every day—and on the front page? I wondered if reading words that inspire thoughtful meditation each morning before checking the stock market returns and the latest crises to befall the world would alter the culture in which I lived?

I was impressed by the power and the beauty of Ooka's words and worried that I might not be able to measure up to his consummate artistry and ability to employ a few words but find exactly the ones that powerfully delivered his message.

Shuntaro Tanikawa was equally extraordinary and inspiring. Author of more than sixty books of poetry, he was also a translator and professor and internationally recognized with many awards and prizes. The English title of his bestselling first book, *Two Billion Light-Years of Solitude*, revealed at once his scholarship and the international stage on which he worked while referring to Marquez's *One Hundred Years of Solitude* and offering a counterpart to his own subsequent volume entitled *Floating the River in Melancholy*. Tanikawa possessed the rare ability to give expression to the depths of the tragic while yet being able to embrace the comic and find reason for laughter in the human condition. The translator of *Peanuts*, author of epic, lyrical, narrative, and satirical verse, he also wrote novels, plays, and songs for radio, television, and films, including "Firebird," the theme song of the eponymous movie. He achieved all this while holding his position as a professor at the Tokyo National University of Fine Arts and Music.

A fourth poet from South Korea, Yong-Jik Kim, was added, making a collaborative of four writers and four languages, as I was responsible for writing both English and French versions. Kim was a professor at Seoul National University and a poet whose work had been published by the Korean Culture and Arts Foundation and whose literary criticism had appeared in *Azalea: The Journal of Korean Literature and Culture*. He received the highest awards not only for his own poetry but also for his translations into Korean and for his sensitive literary analyses of the work of both contemporary and earlier Korean poets.

I felt very small and insignificant and worried that whatever words I might conjure up on the occasion would pale in comparison to those of these grand masters. My doubt and anxiety grew as the date for the August collaboration approached. I had never written in public, and words did not automatically flow from my pen and appear on the page. There were times when I rewrote parts of poems, started anew, and others when the result was deservedly torn into as many small pieces as possible and consigned to the category of appropriately forgotten verses. What if my mind froze? What if I lacked inspiration and nothing flowed from my pen? What if I were to suffer as did Mallarmé, the French poet, who saw himself, a writer, staring at a sheet of white paper, as a swan frozen in an icy lake on a winter's day.

Immobilized, he claimed to suffer from "*la hantise de la page blanche*" (being haunted by the blank page). That might well apply to me! I need not have worried as much as I did because of the kind and gentle welcoming of Tanikawa and Ooka, who assured me that even though poets were known to take hours or even days on occasion to produce a single verse, we would definitely be able to write thirty-six. (In the end, we only wrote twenty-four, but Ooka and Tanikawa pointed out that never before had such a poem been written in four languages at once. They therefore considered the completed twenty-four-verse work a success and declared our mission accomplished.)Well-known international *rengas* include one, which has been acclaimed as the first, by Mexican poet and diplomat and Nobel laureate Octavio Paz; accompanied by Eduardo Sanguinetti, a Genoese poet, professor, and parliamentarian; English poet, professor, and translator Charles Tomlinson; and Jacques Roubaud, a French professor of mathematics, poet, and translator of Lewis Carroll. They had come together in Paris for five days in the spring of 1969 to write an adapted form of *renga*. These fine writers were also experimenting and trying to create something that went beyond linked verse in the shape of an international, poetic dialogue. Their goals were "to see if four voices from the four corners of the world could find a basic harmony. To see if each could remain *I* and *you* at the same time as becoming *Us*. To see what element or common element would come about from this 'United Nations' of poets. To see, in short, what we should hear from this quadrilingual quarter, this international foursome."[1] Their "Parisian project" did not quite achieve the linear and melodic order prescribed by the

1. Octavio Paz, Jacques S. Roubaud, Eduardo Sanguinetti, and Charles Tomlinson, *Renga: A Chain of Poems* (George Braziller, 1971); Charles Tomlinson, "Renga and Renshi: Linked Poems, Linked Traditions," *Agenda Poetry*, vol. 40, 4, autumn/winter 2004, p. 1–10, Broadsheet pdf. https://www.agendapoetry.co.uk/CharlesTomlinson-Renga.pdf.pdf.

Japanese form, resulting in what they themselves termed "counterpoint and polyphony." Each of the four poets returned home after five days and, over the ensuing months, separately composed a series of seven poems, which were then linked by a network of allusions and shared themes, creating a thread that connected the poems of the four writers.

In contrast, in the "Tokyo" *renga* or *renshi*, which we composed in 1991, stanzas were each written sequentially, in response to the preceding verse, as had been the traditional practice dating back to 1356. This provided greater unity in the text and extraordinary dialogue among the authors. However, due to the difficulties of writing a poem in four languages at once, some of the rules, including the number of syllables, had to be dropped. Unlike the comparatively leisurely pace of the Parisian venture, which allowed the authors to continue writing from home after the event, the Tokyo poets were given slightly less than forty-eight hours to complete their project.

In the 1980s, Ooka had pioneered a modernized version of the *renga*, which he called *renshi*. Shuntaro Tanikawa joined him in this creative venture from the outset. They were born in the same year, and their collaborative efforts flourished along with their friendship and obvious respect for each other. Over time the most popular themes for these linked poems were the seasons, love, reminiscence (including grief and nostalgia), travel, and Buddhism. There were normally at least two references to flowers and three to the moon. There should be an allusion to the season and some reference, perhaps metaphorical, to the current events and context at the time of writing, as well as an indication of the geographical location. As we wrote, we were instructed by Ooka about the various rules and reminded to be sure to connect the stanzas and to bring each other back down to reality should poetic enthusiasm carry us away. Each stanza was immediately translated into three other languages and there was much dialogue among the translators and the writers about the choice of words and their explicit and implicit meanings. The poem observed the ancient tradition of three-line stanzas followed by stanzas of five lines.

The principal differences between the Paris and the Tokyo verses were that the Parisian venture was based on the sonnet form and was centred on structure, a rather strict frame, while the Tokyo production was more about process and evolved organically, as each poet added to and responded to the prior stanza. Since the Tokyo *renshi* was written simultaneously in four languages, some of the structural rules were set aside. The Paris texts were written in private by each of the authors, at a distance (each poet having returned to his home), and over an indeterminate amount of time. On the other hand, the Tokyo texts were composed in public with poets, translators, and university staff all present in one room within a compressed time frame. Writers asked each other about words and meaning, and translators clarified their intent at the same time. Ooka acted as teacher and mentor, establishing boundaries and reminding us of rules, whereas Paz left each writer to produce their section, which they subsequently reworked to try to knit them together. Finally, the Paris text remains personal and individual, whereas the Tokyo text is a true dialogue and exchange of thoughts and emotions.

As you read the Tokyo poem, you will notice that it begins with the traditional reference to the season, *Natsu*, the summer. Ooka had asked Tanikawa to begin with a traditional reference to the season and to offer a welcome to the poets who had come from afar to join the session. He did this elegantly, using the word *Natsu*, which is both a woman's name and the season. Since each verse is linked to the one before, the first verse includes a reflection on memories that indicate the past, but are, like the leaves that fall from the trees in the autumn, also the source of new life, and, in this case, literary invention. The memories and trees are picked up in the second stanza. The bamboo trunks play on the leaves and frame the view from the window, but trunks are also the places where memories are stored. The reference to the Canadian maple acknowledges the international welcome and the gentle murmur of their leaves is that of the poets talking, outlining the creative concept and sharing meaning across languages and cultures. Traditionally, the third verse should play on the predecessors and introduce a new thought. Ooka thus translated memories of the past to the concept of time, when humans can create in a space not measured by the clock, a space where we can strive to transcend time and its limits. The fourth verse harkens back to the past we all carry with us as we move to new horizons.

Our understanding of the *renga* tradition was broadened, as Ooka instructed us that the poem must include not only a seasonal word to denote when it was composed but also an indication of the location and what was happening in the world at that time. He provided the place name quite mischievously with the insertion of Tokyo's toad, sitting perplexed atop a construction site. Two large buildings were completed in Tokyo in 1991: the Tokyo Metropolitan Government Building, which was at that time the tallest building in Tokyo, and the Earthtecture Sub-1, built with four stories underground, the street level resembling a rock garden. Either might have bemused Ooka's frog, which is special because it only appears in the summer months and is endemic to Japan. Ooka adds a note of humour with what might perhaps be a subtle reference to Murakami's story, "Super Frog Saves Tokyo." It could also be a way of evoking his own poem, "What Is Poetry #4" in which poetry, like a baby frog, "leaps into time—space—the old pond." On a darker note, it might also refer to Tanikawa's sad meditation on death and aging, on being a person and a writer, on temporality and eternity, which concludes, "Listening to frogs / we fall asleep in futons placed side by side / both 'Me' and I are now the 'sparkling dust of the universe.'" It is an elegant reminder of the ancient poetic form we were imitating, the burgeoning world of tall buildings under construction in 1991, and the fact that what was new to us was actually an ancient tradition. The use of the word toad takes the frog down a notch and reminds the reader and the writers alike of the humility poets should adopt. It was also possibly Ooka's way of gently telling me in verse what he whispered over my shoulder as I bent over my writing at the table where we all sat, that I had perhaps included the galaxies too soon and, according to the rules, the verses should not take flight until the thirty-sixth stanza was in sight. However, he liked the stanza and let it stand, and I resolved to keep my images securely tied to the ground, as can be noted in the verses that followed. It is easy to distinguish the voice of each poet.

Kim's voice is often angry, reflecting the harsh experience of his native land. Tanikawa is Ooka's disciple and translates the rules into reality with a kind, pensive, and wistful, perhaps rueful understanding of the limits and possibilities of human creativity. Ooka is the glue that keeps the writers together, adding a note of humour and emphasizing what we all share as human beings. He reiterates the belief in the power of poetry at the end of the poem, reintroducing hope in response to the frustration expressed by Kim. I think my own voice was perhaps the softest and gentlest. I know I was seeking expressions of beauty that would be understood across international cultures and was picking up on the themes of nature versus culture (the firefly and *Mona Lisa* / nature and art), the depths of human ignorance that make the galaxies shudder, and the power of art to heal and inspire (the stroke of the master's brush dipped in azure dew).

One of the most fascinating features of this project stemmed from the fact that the writers were all readers responding to each other's words and, at the same time, co-creators embroidering each other's text and translators explaining the intended meanings subtly embedded in the choice of expression. At times, the sense can be easily grasped, as for example, in the wildlife leitmotif, including an owl, fireflies, and geese taking flight along with whales singing, but also accompanied by a crab and the toad firmly sitting on the earth. At other moments, it can be heard as dialogue where Kim wonders about the differences that separate people and cultures, and Tanikawa, who responds, reconciling the matter by indicating that perceived differences are superficial, while people are all bound by their profound humanity.

The current events of the day included the World Championships in Athletics that were held at the Olympic Stadium in Tokyo from August 23 to September 1, 1991. Tanikawa nods to them in stanza 12. Stanzas 15 and 21 are references, seen from the perspective of South Korean poet, Yong-Jik Kim, not only to politics in Korea but also to the attempted coup that occurred the very day when we were writing. Walking to the university where we were given a fine room in which to write, we heard the news and read headlines about what was to be known as the failed "August coup" from August 18 to 22, 1991, on the Soviet Parliament by Communist hardliners who were opposed to Gorbachev's reforms. On those August days, writing in relative isolation in Tokyo, we had no inkling of what would follow over the course of the next few months. Kim's concerns for freedom of expression were, however, universal and he wrote on behalf of those in other lands who feared to speak. The failed takeover was indeed the harbinger of a dramatic chapter in world history that saw, within several months, the dissolution of the Soviet Union.

In the local news that captured headlines in August 1991, the DoCoMo company in Tokyo spun off from NTT to take over mobile cellular operations. This is subtly referred to in the third stanza, where analog and digital are juxtaposed as human attempts to capture time, something we can measure but never control. And Ooka admitted that he was particularly fond of the image of the person astride the hands of the analog clock, which he much preferred to its more recent (at that time) digital descendants.

Many stanzas contrast light and darkness, night and day and are punctuated by the constant return to poetic efforts to uplift humanity and to inspire hope and light. Sadly, words fail—they blind the visionary or are absorbed by the darkness that swallows computer graphics, which invade the quiet of the tatami room. Galaxies are unattainable. The fireflies, which can be caught, cease to glow in captivity. And yet, art prevails with the example of the *Mona Lisa*, whose enigmatic smile beams across centuries and continents. Human beings walk, jump, and run even though they cannot move the hands of time. Music reappears throughout the stanzas and like poetry, it may be silenced, not heard at all, or it may announce what Kim presciently imagines, long before the introduction of the term “fake news,” the disinformation provided by the media. At verse 24, the enigmas remain, like hieroglyphs, unsolved. The poets ran out of time that day but maintained solidarity in their belief in the power of art over centuries. They wisely left the conclusion to the next generation of poets, who will be reborn to tread again on the paths of poetry and whose brushes may be once more “dipped in azure dew and capture the velvet sigh of the mountain.”

When we finished writing the poem, the poets met with the literary critics and read the work in Japanese, Korean, English, and French. You may listen to this reading, which was recorded at that time. The link may be found at the end of this volume.

The Poem

1
Please call me Natsu (summer)
I will welcome you, clad in white clouds
Dyed with leaves
And entertain you with memories
Like a mulch of rotten leaves

Shuntaro

2
Memories fall away like years
Framed in bamboo trunks
Or in maples who speak softly among themselves

Roseann

3
There are people slowly circling, riding
The second hand of an analog clock
There are people gasping, jumping
The steps of a digital clock
While time sleeps outside it all

Makoto

4
The man walking to the sea
Is accompanied by ancient tales
The moon leans long

Yong-Jik

5
Swallowing several million plankton at one gulp
The whale begins to sing:
His leisurely melody
Does not reach the ears
Of the youths on the beach

Shuntaro

6
The planets observe jealously
The red void of the poem on the waves
Which overflow the banks of meaning

Roseann

7
The virgin breast the hand of love
Touches for the first time
The bulb within the springtime earth
Stretches for the first time
Swelling, bursting, ah the joy!

Makoto

8
The Queen of Sheba returns to life
A basket in her left hand
Will she fill it with the owl's hoot?

Yong-Jik

9
The bas-relief decorating the temple doorway
Bears its enigma like the pyramids in the blind desert
Silent like the prism which separates
Into colours the amber heat
Of the sun's creation

Roseann

10
The too-bright light of day
Steals the subtle shadow of all objects
I, an artist, choose the night.

Makoto

11
I want to walk alone
Like a fawn along the mountain path
Though the wind sleeps and the starlight fades,
The red warmth of the blood in my heart
Stirs my belief in living while I walk alone

Yong-Jik

12
In the stadium nearby
They strive to jump higher
Some devote half a life to speed

Shuntaro

13
Garlands of words and liminal ribbons
Dance in the poet's grove
Hope is born in a stream of ink
The horizons meld into the skies
Galaxies shudder

Roseann

14
Under the starry sky
Atop the construction site's excavated pile
Aroused from sleep, perplexed, sits Tokyo's toad

Makoto

15
Shall I be a popular writer?
Or the mist that is the backdrop of his stage?
Forswearing demonstrations, meetings, ideologies,
procedures, partition, taxes, Seoul, Pyeongyang,
colonies, anti-imperialism
To float across the barbed wire of the DMZ
Shall I be the mist that comes and goes at will?

Yong-Jik

16
Being on the menu doesn't guarantee the taste
Korean kimchi, Japanese takuan, Canadian corn relish,
Differentiating, we unconsciously share

Shuntaro

17
A Mesopotamian proverb reads—
He with naught to call his own
Shall sleep a far deeper sleep
Than he who clings to gold and silver…
Written in three-thousand B.C. if memory serves

Makoto

18
In a vase, fireflies
Refuse to shine
But the Mona Lisa smiles yet behind her glass

Roseann

19
The monsters of computer graphics
Have chased away the familiar ghosts:
Night after night, poor bits of fluff
From the dim corners of the tatami room
Are swallowed up by a big black hole.

Shuntaro

20
I take a hammer, a great big fellow
And smash the wall of language with all my strength
Breaking the poem to see the essence of things

Yong-Jik

21
The disciples of Zen reach the ultimate pass
"Kill the Buddha" comes the order
"Kill the Masters"
Then from the footprints of the strangled dead
Blossom flowers, and the world rises again

Makoto

22
I thought I heard the wild geese in the marsh
But it was the mountain heaving a velvet sigh
A stroke of the master's brush, dipped in azure dew

Roseann

23
And music is never out of hearing
Reproaching, excusing all warnings of stagnation
    and impasses
Yet any groan of suffering
Can become a delicate song
In the deep twists and turns of the human ear

Shuntaro

24
As a harp welcoming the autumn
As a crab dwelling in the cove
Like a lie, like the headline

Yong-Jik

Le poème

1
Prière de m'appeler Natsu (été)
Je vous accueillerai, vêtue de nuages blancs
Teints de feuilles
Et je vous entretiendrai de souvenirs
Semblables à l'humus de feuilles mortes

Shuntaro

2
Les souvenirs tombent comme les années
Encadrés de troncs de bambou
Ou d'érables qui se parlent doucement

Roseann

3
Des gens tournent lentement à cheval
Sur l'aiguille d'une horloge
D'autres halètent, sautent
Les marches d'une horloge numérique
Tandis que le temps dort, loin de tout

Makoto

4
L'homme se dirigeant vers la mer
Est accompagné de contes anciens
La lune se penche longuement Yong-Jik

5
Avalant des masses de plancton d'une seule goulée
La baleine se met à chanter
Sa mélodie oisive
N'atteint pas les oreilles
Des jeunes sur la plage

Shuntaro

6
Les planètes observent jalousement
Le creux rouge du poème sur les vagues
Qui débordent les berges du sens

Roseann

7
Le sein vierge que la main de l'amour
Touche pour la première fois
Le bulbe dans la terre printanière
S'étire pour la première fois
S'enfle, éclate, ah ! quelle joie

Makoto

8
La reine de Saba revient à la vie
Un panier à la main gauche
L'emplira-t-elle du cri du hibou ? Yong-Jik

9
Le bas-relief ornant le portique du temple
Porte son énigme comme les pyramides du désert aveugle
Silencieux comme le prisme qui sépare
En couleurs la chaleur ambrée
De la création solaire

Roseann

10
La trop brillante lumière du jour
Vole les ombres subtiles de tous les objets
Moi, l'artiste, je choisis la nuit

Makoto

11
Je veux me promener seul
Comme un faon le long d'un sentier montagneux
Malgré le vent qui dort et les étoiles qui s'éteignent
La rouge chaleur du sang dans mon cœur
Me donne envie de croire à la vie en me promenant seul

Yong-Jik

12
Dans le stade voisin
Ils s'efforcent de sauter plus haut
Certains consacrent la moitié de leur vie à la vitesse

Shuntaro

13
Des guirlandes de mots et des rubans liminaires
Dansent dans le bosquet des poètes
L'espoir naît dans un ruisseau d'encre
Les horizons touchent aux cieux,
Les galaxies basculent

Roseann

14
Sous le ciel étincelant d'étoiles
Sur l'amas de pierres déterrées du chantier
Perplexe et à peine éveillé, voilà le crapaud de Tokyo

Makoto

15
Serai-je un écrivain populaire ?
Ou la brume, l'arrière-plan de sa scène ?
Abandonnant manifestations, réunions, idéologies,
procédures, division, impôts, Séoul, Pyongyang,
colonies, anti-impérialisme
Pour voguer à travers les fils barbelés de la zone démilitarisée
Serai-je la brume qui va et vient à sa guise ?

Yong-Jik

16
Figurer au menu ne garantit pas la saveur
Kimchi coréen, takuan japonais, relish de maïs canadienne
En distinguant, nous partageons sans le savoir

Shuntaro

17
Un proverbe mésopotamien dit :
Celui qui n'a rien à son nom
Dormira plus profondément
Que celui qui tient à son or et à son argent
Écrit en l'an trois mille avant J.-C., si la mémoire est bonne

Makoto

18
Dans un bocal les lucioles
Refusent de briller
Mais la Joconde sourit toujours derrière sa vitre

Roseann

19
Les monstres du dessin informatisé
Ont chassé les fantômes familiers :
Nuit après nuit, de minables moutons de poussière
Des sombres coins de la salle tatami
Se font avaler par un énorme trou noir

Shuntaro

20
Je saisis un marteau, un énorme machin
Et je fracasse le mur de la langue de toute ma force
Brisant le poème pour voir l'essence des choses

Yong-Jik

21
Les disciples de Zen atteignent l'étape ultime
« Tuez le Bouddha » arrive l'ordre
« Tuez les Maîtres »
Puis, des empreintes de pas des morts étranglés
Des fleurs bourgeonnent, et le monde renaît

Makoto

22
Je croyais entendre les oies sauvages dans le marais
Mais c'était la montagne qui poussait un soupir de velours,
Effet du pinceau du maître, imbu de rosée azurée

Roseann

23
Et la musique n'est jamais loin de l'ouïe
Elle accuse, elle excuse tous les avertissements de l'inertie et des impasses
Mais le moindre gémissement devient une mélodie délicate
Dans les profondeurs tordues
De l'oreille humaine

Shuntaro

24
Comme une harpe qui accueille l'automne
Comme un crabe qui demeure dans l'anse
Tel un mensonge, tels les gros titres de journaux

Yong-Jik

詩

1
私を夏と呼んで下さい
草木に染められた白い雲をまとって
あなたを迎え
腐葉土のような記憶で
私はあなたをもてなしましょう

俊太郎

2
思い出は年月のように散りつづける
竹にふちどられ
ささやき交わす楓にふちどられ

ロゼアン

3
アナログ時計の秒針に乗って
同じ場所をゆっくり回っている人もいる
デジタル時計の数字の階段を
あえぎあえぎジャンプしている人もいる
ときはその外側で眠っているのに

信

4
海へ行く人に
昔話がお供する
その時つきは大きな歩幅で傾く

金容稷

5
数百万のプランクトンをひと呑みにして
鯨は歌い始める
そのゆったりした旋律は
浜辺の若者たちの耳には
とどかない

俊太郎

6
惑星たちはねたましげに見守る
意味の岸からあふれ出た波に浮かぶ
詩の赤いからっぽ

ロゼアン

7
恋する手が
はじめて触れにやってくる乳房
大地の下で
はじめて今年の伸びをする球根
膨張し破壊することの何という歓喜

信

8
再びシバの女王は蘇る
左手には手籠一つ
ふくろうの声を盛ろうとするのか

金容稷

9
寺院の戸口を飾る浮彫——
茫々たる砂漠に立つピラミッドの群のように謎めいて
また太陽の創る琥珀色の熱を
さまざまな色に分解する
プリズムさながら音もなく

ロゼアン

10
明るすぎる昼の光は
物体の微妙な影を奪ってしまう
だから私は　画家として　夜を選ぶ

信

11
一人で歩きたい
山路を行く子鹿のように
風眠り　星の光かくれても
胸にはあたたかい虹の血
独り歩き　人生を信じる

金容稷

12
すぐ近くの競技場には
高く跳ぶことを競い
早く走ることに半生を捧げる人々もいて

俊太郎

13
言葉の花束と意識の堺のリボンが
詩人たちの木立で眠る
インクの小川に希望が生まれ
地平線には空に溶け
銀河は身震いする

ロゼアン

14
星空の下　掘り返された建築現場
瓦礫の上には　困惑しきって
東京のヒキガエル

信

15
大衆作家にでもなろうか
彼の舞台の背景の霧にでもなろうか
デモなんか、会議なんか、イデオロギー、手続き、
　　分断、税金なんか、ソウルも、平壌も、
　　植民地も、反帝も、 そんなも、
　　のなどかかわりなく、鉄条網、休戦ライン、
自由気ままに行き来する
霧にでもなろうか

金容稷

16
メニューは必ずしも味を保証しないが
キムチ・タクアン・コーンレリッシュ
比べることで私たちは気づかずに頒ちあう

俊太郎

17
メソポタミアの諺にいわく——
金や銀を抱えこんでる人々よりも
無一文の人の方が
夜ごとぐっすり眠れるだろうと. . . . .
たしかにあれは紀元前三千年の諺だった

信

18
花瓶の中では蛍は光ることを拒む
だがモナリザはガラスの壁のむこうで
なおもほほえむ

ロゼアン

19
ＣＧの描き出す怪物が
なつかしい幽霊を追い出してしまった
座敷の小暗い片隅の
哀れな綿埃は毎夜
ブラック・ホールに吸いこまれる

俊太郎

20
ハンマー　そのでっかいやつを握る
精いっぱい言語の壁をぶちこわし
詩を打ち倒して事物の実体を見

金容稷

21
禅家の修行は
ゆきつくところ仏を殺し
祖師を殺せと命じた
しめ殺された仏や祖師の足跡から
華はまた開き世界は起つのだ

信

22
湿地でガンの声が聞こえると思ったら
山がビロードの嘆息をついていた
紺色の霧を含んだ巨匠の一刷毛

ロゼアン

23
そしていつも音楽が聞こえている
渋滞の警報の非難と弁解の音楽
だがどんな苦しみの呻きすら時に
微妙な歌. . . . .
人の耳の曲がりくねった窪みで

俊太郎

24
秋をむかえるハーブの如く
入江に住む蟹の如く
ウソのように、事件のように

金容稷

시

1
나를 여름이라 불러주오
초목에 물든 흰 구름을 걸치고
그대를 맞아
부엽토 (腐葉土)와 같은 기억으로
나는 그대를 대접하겠소

Shuntaro

2
추억은 세월처럼 흩어진다
대나무 테두리에 싸여
속삭이는 단풍나무에 둘러싸여

Roseann

3
아나로그 시계의 초침을 타고
같은 장소를 천천히 돌고 있는 사람도 있다
디지탈 시계의 숫자판 계단을
헐떡이며 뛰어오르는 사람도 있다
시간은 그 바깥에서 잠들어 있는데

Makoto

4
바다로 가는 사람에게
옛날 이야기가 따라간다
달은 그럴 때 꽤 많이 기운다

용직

5
수백만개의 플랑크톤을 꿀꺽 삼키고
고래는 노래부르기 시작한다
그 느긋한 선율은
해변의 젊은이들 귀에는
들리지 않는다

Shuntaro

6
혹성들은 부러운 듯 지켜본다
의미의 언덕을 흘러 넘쳐 파도에 뜬
시의 빨간 껍질을

Roseann

7
사랑하는 손이
처음으로 만지러 오는 유방
대지 아래서
올해 처음으로 몫을 움틔우는 구근 (球根)
팽창하여 파열하는 이 멋지 환희

Makoto

8
다시 시바여왕은 소생한다
왼손에는 광우리 하나
그 속에 부엉이 소리를 담으려나

용직

9
사원 (寺院) 의 입구를 장식하는 부(조浮彫)-''
청맹과니 사막에 선 피라밋들과도 같이 신비로운
태양이 빚어내는 빨간 빛 열을
갖가지 빛깔로 분해한다
마치 프리즘인양 소리도 없이

Roseann

10
너무 밝은 대낮의 빛은
물체의 미묘한 그림자를 뺏어 버린다
그래서 나는 밤을 택한다

Makoto

11
혼자서 걷고 싶다
산길을 가는 아기사슴처럼
바람이 잠들고 별빛이 숨어도
가슴에는 따뜻한 진한 빨간색 피
혼자서 걸으며 인생을 믿고 싶다

용직

12
바로 옆 경기장에선
높이뛰기를 겨루고
빨리 달리기에 일생을 거는 사람들도 있고

Shuntaro

13
언어의 꽃다발과 의식의 경지에 매단 리본이
시인들의 숲에서 춤춘다
잉크가 흐르는 시내에 희망이 태어나
지평선은 하늘에 녹고
은하는 몸부림 친다

Roseann

14
별밤에 파헤쳐진 건축현장
자갈 위에는 당혹삼에 빠진
동경 (도쿄)의 두꺼비

Makoto

15
대중작가나 될까
그 무대 배경으로 쓴 안개나 될까
데모 같은 것, 회의 같은 것, 이데오로기, 수속, 분단,
    세금 같은 것, 서울도 평양도, 식민지도,
    반제도 反帝
그런 것 모두 무관하게 철조망 휴전선 마음대로
넘나드는 안개나 될까

용직

16
메뉴가 꼭 맛을 보증하지는 않지만
김치, 타쿠앙, 콘 레리쉬
견주어 보는 것으로 우리들은 의식않고 서로를나눈다

Shuntaro

17
메소포타미아 속담에 이르기를
금, 은에 파묻혀 사는 사람들보다
무일푼인 사람이
밤마다 푹 잠들 수 있을 거라고
분명 그건 기원전 3천년의 속담이었다

Makoto

18
꽃병 속에서 반디는 반짝이길 거부한다
하지만 모나리자는 액자속에서
여전히 미소짓는다

Roseann

19
컴퓨터 그래픽이 그려내는 정물이
친근한 유령을 몰아내 버렸다
응접실 어슴푸레한 귀퉁이의
가련한 먼지는 매일 밤
블랙 홀로 빨려 들어간다

Shuntaro

20
해머. 그 큰 것을 잡는다
힘있게 언어의 벽을 깨고
시를 타도해서 사물의 실체를 본다

용직

21
선가의 수행은
궁극에는 부처를 죽이고
조사를 죽이라고 명했다
목졸려 죽은 부처와 조사의 발자취에서
꽃은 다시 피고 세계는 일어서는 것이다

Makoto

22
습지에서 기러기 울음소리가 들리는가 했더니
산이 빌로도의 한숨을 쉬고 있었다
쪽빛 이슬을 머금은 장인의 일필

Roseann

23
그리고는 늘 음악이 들려온다
교통체증경보의 비난과 변명의 음악
하지만 어떤 괴로움의신음소리조차 때로는
미묘한 노래
우리 귀에 오묘한 깊이로

Shuntaro

24
가을에 만든 하프처럼
강 입구에 사는 게처럼
'거짓말처럼, 사건처럼

용직

The Poem as Performance

Participants

The Convenor

Toru Haga, an eminent professor and scholar of Japanese literature, taught at Tokyo National University and later became president of Kyoto University of the Arts. He was author of many acclaimed studies, including *Land of Poetry, Land of Poets, Pax Tokugawana: The Cultural Flowering of Japan 1603-1853, Arts and Culture of Japan from the Eighteenth to the Twentieth Century*, and work on *manga*. His focus on international thinking and cultural exchange was evident in *Masterpieces on Japan by Foreign Ambassadors*, which he edited with Shoichi Saeki. Among his last projects were *Writing of Diplomats* and *The Peach Blossom Spring in East Asian Literature and Art.* He was president of the International Comparative Literature Association and was responsible for the major conference in Tokyo in 1991 as well as for the collaborative writing of the *renga*.

The Poets

Makoto Ooka, poet, novelist, journalist, and critic, authored over 250 volumes of work, taught at Meiji University, the Tokyo National University of Fine Arts and Music and lectured at Harvard, Princeton, and the Collège de France. He served as director of the Japan Artists Association, chair of the Japan Contemporary Poets Society, chair of the Japan P.E.N. Club, and chair of the Japanese Arts Academy. He received the Cultural Merit Award, was inducted into the Japanese Arts Academy, and was made Officier (Officer) in l'Ordre des Arts et des Lettres de France. He was awarded the prestigious International Golden Wreath at the Struga Poetry Evenings.

Shuntaro Tanikawa, poet, translator, novelist, and professor, wrote over sixty volumes of poetry, including *Floating the River in Melancholy*, which was translated by William Elliott and won the American Book Award. His first novel, *Two Billion Light-Years of Solitude* (1952) is still widely read. He translated Charles Schulz's *Peanuts* as well as the Mother Goose stories and Hans Christian Andersen's tales for children. His works, such as *Coca-Cola Lessons*, *Listening to Mozart*, and *Ordinary People* are well known. He wrote songs for television, radio, and film of which some, like "Firebird," are the theme song for the eponymous film. He wrote epic, lyrical, narrative, and satirical verse and visited every continent except Antarctica. He was a professor at the Tokyo National University of Fine Arts and Music and was awarded the prestigious International Golden Wreath Prize at the Struga Poetry Evenings.

Yong-Jik Kim, professor in the Department of Korean Language and Literature in the Faculty of the Humanities at Seoul National University in South Korea, poet, and translator of Chinese verse, published several volumes on modern Korean poets, poetry, and the analysis of poetry principles. He received many awards, including the March 3 Culture Prize, the Republic of Korea Literature Prize, the Sejong Culture Prize, and the Modern Literature Prize. He was president of the Literary Translation Institute of Korea, the Modern Korean Literature Society, the Korean Comparative Literature Association, and the Korean Society for Poetics.

Roseann O'Reilly Runte, professor of French and comparative literature, author of three volumes of poetry in French, editor and author of scholarly works, president of several universities and of the Canada Foundation for Innovation, received the Prix François Coppée from the Académie française, the Ordre des Palmes académiques and l'Ordre du Mérite of France, the Ordre de la Couronne of Belgium, and Fellowship in the Royal Society of Canada. She is an Officer in the Order of Canada.

The Musicians

Richard "Dick" Armin, Canadian cellist who studied with Starker, Markevitch, and Silva, taught at York University and was known for his innovations, which included the digital interface of instruments played through speakers. He played electronic string instruments and performed with the Lighthouse Band and the group Les Amis.

Oliver Schroer, a Canadian violinist and prolific composer, studied at York University and taught music in British Columbia. He recorded ten CDs and performed across Europe and North America, including at the Lincoln Center in New York. He produced or performed on one hundred recorded albums.

Casey Sokol, pianist, studied at the State University of New York, California Institute of the Arts, and York University, where he shares his talents, specializing in piano, musical improvisation, and musicianship. He also studied at the American Society for Eastern Arts at Mills College. He continues to perform in concerts around the world, in music festivals, and on radio and television.

Robert Bick, classical flautist, spent a decade performing and recording in Europe and across North America. He played with the Gaillard Ensemble, a classical music quartet and among his well-known recordings was "The Romantic Flute." A legend in Canadian business, he played a strong role in the success of his family's farm and went on to a brilliant career in business, serving as CEO and later chair of the Evolving Gold Corp.

David Mott, baritone saxophonist, graduated from the Berkley College of Music with a Master of Music and a Master of Musical Arts and a PhD in Music from Yale University. He was a professor of music at York University and remains a professional musician and composer. He also has a seventh level black belt in karate and in his spare time runs his own Dojo in Toronto.

The Artist

Sylviane de Roquebrune, artist, curator of art for York University and director of the Art Gallery at Glendon College in Toronto, fully embraced this project and created a beautiful painting for each of the stanzas, dedicating the use of the gallery and, above all, her time, creativity, and care in working with the dancers to choreograph and produce the performance. With bachelors' and graduate degrees in art, art-education, and studio art, Sylviane de Roquebrune is a multimedia artist and professor from Quebec who has worked in Abu Dhabi, Canada, and the United States and has collaborated with the Louvre, the Guggenheim, and the British Museum.

The Dancers

Uno Man, a leading Japanese dancer and choreographer, studied Butoh, the classical dance form, before creating his own style of modern, oriental choreography. Prior to his North American tour, which opened with the *renga,* he had been performing for two decades with his company in Asia, the United States, and Europe. With his internationally acclaimed company known for the beauty and energy of its work, he has collaborated with the musicians, artist, and poets to create a specially choreographed performance of the poem.

The Contributing Author and Translator

Ted Goossen began his studies of Japanese at the age of nineteen, discovering his passion for Japan's language and literature. He received his PhD from the University of Toronto and has taught in the Department of Contemporary Literary Studies at the University of Tokyo and at York University, where he was instrumental in establishing East Asian studies and where he is currently emeritus professor of contemporary Japanese literature. He is well known for his exceptional translations of Hiromi Kawakami's books, including *People from My Neighborhood, Dragon Palace*, and *The Third Love*, as well as Haruki Murakami's *Hear the Wind Sing, Pinball, 1973, Men Without Women,* and *The Strange Library* and Naoya Shiga's *Reconciliation.* He is editor of the literary annual *Monkey* (formerly *Monkey Business)*, which features new writing from Japan in English translation and is editor of the *Oxford Book of Japanese Short Stories.* He has been honoured by Japan with the award of the Order of the Rising Sun.

The Translators

Bio Aikawa, born in Toyama, Japan, was just fourteen when she first visited Canada and was enchanted with its natural beauty and dynamic culture. Determined to return and motivated by a lasting curiosity and her mother's unwavering support, she earned a doctorate in biological sciences from Carleton University and has since worked for the Government of Canada in the Ministries of Health and the Environment.. She is a proud Canadian by choice and Japanese by birth. She is known for her volunteer service in the Ottawa community, where she teaches children respect and discipline through the martial arts.

Michiko Aikawa was born eight years after renowned poets Shuntaro Tanikawa and Makoto Ooka. While studying law at Nagoya University, she was a classmate of Tanikawa's cousin, an early connection to a world of ideas and ideals. As a faculty member at Toyama University, from 1971 to 2005, she was a trailblazer, not only through her academic achievement but also through the courage and compassion she brought to all she did and those she touched, especially her students, who continue to draw inspiration from her enduring legacy.

Hyounjeong Yoo, professor of Korean language and culture at Carleton University, has written on language acquisition and on Korean cinema. Her work includes translations between Japanese and Korean as well as English and Korean.

Theresa Hyun is professor of Korean studies in the humanities program at York University. Dr. Hyun previously taught for a decade at Kyunghee University in Korea. She holds a PhD in French and Medieval Studies from the University of Iowa and in addition to numerous articles on translation and cultural identity, she has written three major books: *Writing Women in Korea: Translation and Feminism in the Colonial Period*, *Translation and Modernization* (with José Lambert), and *Translation and Early Modern Korean Literature.*

The Photographers

Cylla von Tiedemann is world-renowned for her work as a photographer of the performing arts, in which she captures the movement of dancers. She was a photographer for the National Ballet in Canada and for Yo-Yo Ma's Silk Road Project. She has lectured at the Toronto Metropolitan University, Sheridan College, Concordia University, and the

Canadian Centre for Photography. The National Arts Centre produced a book of her work: *The Dance Photographs of Cylla von Tiedemann.*

Jean-Marc Carisse was the official photographer to three Canadian prime ministers. His stellar career is documented through books and exhibits dedicated to his work and is illustrated by his uncanny ability to be in the right spot at the perfect moment and to record it with clarity and elegance. Recipient of the Library and Archives Canada Scholar Award and the Queen Elizabeth II Golden Jubilee Medal, he is as well known as are many of his famous subjects, among whom was Mother Teresa.

The Stage Manager

Michel Charbonneau, director of the Glendon Theatre at York University, dedicated his talent and efforts to coordinate the many actors and technical aspects of this production and assure the technical support required.

The Sound Technician

Nick Schofield is a Canadian musician, audio engineer, and ambassador of ambient music. He has a Bachelor of Fine Arts in Electro-acoustic Studies from Concordia University and now works as the technical director of the SAW Centre in Ottawa as well as at Debaser's Pique Festival. A practising artist, Nick has released many solo and group albums, which have often been reviewed by *The Guardian*, *CBC*, *Q*, and *The Toronto Star,* among others. He actively performs in concert and has appeared at the National Arts Centre, La Place des Arts, the Getty Center in Los Angeles, and National Sawdust in New York.

The Sponsors and Contributors

The Japan Foundation and **Norio Furushima**, executive director of the Japan Foundation, worked diligently, with intelligence and creativity, twenty-four hours a day to make the event a success. Furushima was ably assisted by **Kathleen Yukishige**, who actively helped to develop the event.

The Consulate General of Japan in Toronto, and particularly **Junichi Otaka,** the cultural attaché, whose active, creative, and dedicated service to the realization of the *renshi* project contributed immensely to its success.

Professor Kogi Kawamoto, professor of comparative literature and culture at the University of Tokyo, a member of the Japan Academy, brought his wife and daughter from Japan to accompany him to the program. He supported the work of the team, interfacing with poets, dancers, and musicians. He is best known for his books, such as *The Poetics of Japanese Verse,* and his thoughtful essays included in, for example, *Cybernetic Ghosts: Literature in the Age of Theory and Technology.*

Professor Takayo Kano made it possible for the poets and translators to be warmly welcomed to Aoyama Gakuin Women's Junior College in Tokyo, where the poem was composed and joined the group in Toronto for the performance. Professor Kano, a graduate of the University of Tokyo, is president of the Japan Association of University Women and has served as president of Kwassui Women's University in Nagasaki and of Aoyama Gakuin.

Michel Charbonneau, director of the theatre at Glendon College, hosted the dancers, poets, and musicians and juggled the needs of artists from different cultures and countries who all spoke different languages.

Mr. Chung-ha Yoon, consul general of the Republic of Korea, and **Ms. Young Ju Park Kim** contributed several artistic designs used in the performance.

We thank the **Japan Foundation**, the **Consulate General of Japan**, **Glendon College**, and **York University** for their support and contributions, which made the *renshi* event possible.

The Event and the Program

Imagine you have just taken your seat in the Glendon College Theatre. The stage floor appears to be covered with autumn leaves that have fallen from the trees outside. Toward the back of the stage hangs a white screen.

The stage lights up and the quiet hum of conversation among the audience is hushed in expectation. The poem is read through in Japanese, English, French, and Korean by the poets who stand at a microphone just below the stage, facing the audience. Projected on the screen are the images of paintings created for each of the stanzas, intertwining the visual work and the word.

Then softly, music begins to float delicately on the air, as one instrument at a time picks up the narrative thread. Like the words, the music is the work of individual musicians who each represent the voice of one of the poets and who have, reflecting the *renshi* format, linked their musical compositions both to the whole and to the preceding stanza. The musicians are scattered, like the leaves, but rather than sitting on the stage, they are located throughout the audience, reducing the boundary between spectacle and spectator. The music evokes the images in the interlocking stanzas of the poem. In turn, these images are represented in the abstract paintings, which have been created for each stanza and are now projected on a drape, which acts as a screen at the back of the stage.

In quiet stillness, the leaves appear to move ever so slightly. The audience begins to focus its attention on the luxuriously scattered leaves as dancers slowly and gracefully arise from the blanket of leaves. Clad in white leotards, they move in deliberate and disciplined slow motion, each responding to the music of one instrument, until they move together to envelop themselves in the white drape. When the dancers unfurl themselves and detach from the white screen, which floats down to join the leaves on the stage floor, their white garb becomes the screen against which the paintings are projected. The movements of the dancers have essentially fused with the art and the music, and all have become one. The poets read with the music, which emanates from the musicians seated in the audience. With graceful flourishes, the dancers bow, offering in this final gesture a performance of linked poetry in which music and dance, art and poetry are bound together, making it possible to experience the dialogue, not only of poets united across oceans and cultures but of the arts that can at once portray individual meaning and a modest symphonic synesthesia. We hoped to create a little bit of magic that might engage the audience in a thoughtful consideration of the possibilities of extending and combining the arts, a meditation on meaning and purpose, on the differences and similarities of nations and languages, art and nascent technology, and a moment of beauty in which nature and culture come together.

The Collaborative Creation

Imagine an explosion of creative energy coming together from all corners of the globe and meeting to create a new work of art that combines music, dance, visual art, and literature. A softly warm fall day on the lovely campus of Glendon College had spread a welcome map of fall leaves of every colour across the grounds. A bit like the poets who came together from around the world, the artist, photographers, dancers, technicians, poets, and the impromptu creative directors and stage manager and staff who laid aside their normal employment to assume these important roles met for the first time several days before the performance. The process they followed involved equal doses of innovation and patience. Like the poets before them who spoke four different languages and came from different continents and cultures, the interdisciplinary artists were each communicating in the language of their art—music, dance, or painting—and the "rules" of their medium were stretched to the limit by the technology of the day and by the dialogue among the artists. Like the poets, they had an extremely compressed timeline. October 10 at 8:00 p.m., the show would go on!

The musicians were busy testing the sound and the possibilities of the space. Might they be less "the spectacle" than "participants in the spectacle with the audience"? The dancers, now that they had seen the space and listened to the music, were occupied with re-choreographing the production. The poets were discussing the way they would contribute. Would the entire poem be read at the beginning and at the end? Who would substitute for those who did not make it? Everyone was scurrying madly about. A torn costume, safety pins, duct tape, a bulb for the projector, and maps of the campus, tickets, and publicity. Students and faculty and members of the academic, diplomatic, and neighbouring communities, last-minute recruits all, joined in creating the show and in making it come together.

At one particularly difficult moment, which involved imagining what should be a dramatic opening for the show, we decided to break the tension by taking everyone outside for a walk. The dancers were particularly enchanted by the carpet of leaves that had fallen from the trees. They wanted such a carpet on the stage. This was no problem at all. The campus gardener provided bags and students blithely filled them with the now-precious stage material, scattering the leaves across the stage floor exactly as the dance troupe desired.

There were moments when everyone was very tired, and it seemed as if the show would not come together in time. However, it did and while it was simple in essence, it was also complex in coordinating so many people from different disciplines who had not previously worked as a team.

The show materialized to the delight of all, bringing together three nations and four art forms—dance, poetry, music, and painting. Leading artists from Japan, Korea, and Canada shared their talents and their passion to produce a multilingual event. In composing the music, the musicians followed the alternating stanza format, and their notes resonated with the words. The dancers' movements were harmonized with the music as, stepping into the coloured light of the images projected on the drape, they themselves became one with the artwork that was being shown on the backdrop. They danced within the glow of the projected paintings, becoming part of the art, moving in synchrony with the music and the words.

Ever since, people have asked for more performances or a film, for similar experiences involving other texts and art forms. There was indeed something very special about the production. It was ahead of its time. Today there are many opportunities to mix media and international talent not only with professional actors but with a seemingly unlimited supply of global talent. Yet, despite the advances of technology and the addition of new styles of composition, this project stands out as a rare example of an international, multilingual, multimedia production—a true dialogue of the arts.

Imagining the Process

Imagine how the concept was born. It did not occur *sui generis* but was an idea that crept over me, bit by bit, until I really am not certain where it began. Like the poem, it was the result of collaborative inspiration.

When I returned to Toronto from Tokyo in August 1991, I spoke enthusiastically about the *renshi* experience with my colleagues and friends, who encouraged me to think about presenting the poem to the public in Toronto. I began to imagine a performance of the poem that went beyond the written and spoken word to include music. That was when I contacted several musicians who agreed to join in the project. They assembled a group of some of the most talented artists of the day to compose and perform the work. I then went to the Japan Foundation to see if they might be able to assist in funding a presentation. This would involve bringing the poets to Toronto. They agreed and indicated that the dance troupe, Uno Man, was coming to North America to perform in October. Uno Man agreed, at their behest, to choreograph the poem and perform a dance as part of their tour. I sought help from Sylviane de Roquebrune, the director of the Glendon Art Gallery, and she was instantly inspired, enthusiastic, and totally committed to the project. She painted a work for each stanza and persuaded Cylla von Tiedemann to photograph the paintings to be used in creating slides that could be shown in the performance. Ted Goossen and Theresa Hyun enthusiastically joined in the collaborative effort and involved many colleagues and students. The dean of Glendon College, Yvette Schmidt, provided invaluable assistance in gathering volunteers. The Consul General of Japan was extremely generous in asking his staff to dedicate their knowledge and efficiency to helping the volunteers from the Japan Foundation, as we all rolled up our sleeves and worked together.

The production was entirely the work of volunteers. The poets and artists offered their time and talent. Family, friends, and students joined staff to ensure that every detail was in place, and all came together. Looking back, I marvel at how professional the production appeared, and I attribute that to the talent, time, and dedication of the artists and the community. I still can feel the shiver of anticipation and the breathless murmur of awe as the dancers rose from the leaves to move in perfect coordination with the music, images, and words. I am always reminded of the power of art to bring people of the world together and the power of the people to create beauty. May this *renshi* find its way to your heart and mind, and may you join me in commemorating the talent of these great masters and extraordinary artists.

Casey Sokol has graciously shared his improvised piece, which is reminiscent of the music created for the event. You are invited to listen to it on your device by scanning the following QR code.

In addition, the voices of the poets, entering the room in Tokyo after completing the poem, explaining what they had accomplished, reading their words and sharing their camaraderie and a bit of their thought process before a live audience were saved and, thanks to the restoration and care of Nick Schofield, are available by scanning the following QR code.

Canadian artist, Sylviane de Roquebrune, created a painting for each stanza of the poem. These works were photographed and projected on the white background against which the dancers, wearing white, performed in Toronto. The paintings were subsequently sold or given to the poets and, unfortunately, only two could be located. With the permission of the artist and the owner, they have been reproduced in part on the front and back cover of this volume.

We thank the University of Ottawa Press for accommodating the request to include the artwork and S. Gordon Harwood, Meg Beckel, Whitney Fox, Suzanne Gumpert, Pat Bailey, George Addy, and Lyse Marchand for their advice and Jean-Marc Carisse for his artistry in capturing and reproducing so the palette so perfectly. I am grateful to Danika Gourgon, Mireille Piché, Maryse Cloutier, Martin Llewellyn and their colleagues, and Yoriko Aizu, who have all dedicated their openness, creative energies, and their patient efforts to producing this small book that includes text in four languages, art, and music.

Coda

When their Majesties, the Emperor and Empress of Japan, visited Ottawa on July 6, 2009, they stopped at Carleton University, where they were delighted to meet our students who were studying Japanese and who were deeply honoured to be able to greet the Emperor and Empress in Japanese. I had the great privilege of presenting to them a small scroll with one of the stanzas from the poem.

Gratitude

I am personally grateful to the Japan Foundation for its support of this project and in bringing the choreographer and his dancers to Toronto over thirty years ago and to Uno Man for choreographing and performing the poem on October 11, 1991. That support has continued today and Noriko Yamamoto and the Japan Foundation have once more offered invaluable advice and assistance.

I thank the Ambassador of Japan to Canada, His Excellency Kanji Yamanouchi, for encouraging me to ensure that this page of Japanese Canadian history and the sharing of cultural expression will be enjoyed yet today, adding to the international understanding so needed by the world.

Duo

A New Imprint Dedicated to Literary Works and Ideas

Duo presents works of fiction and non-fiction, in French and in English, as well as in Indigenous languages, from established writers and emerging talents. It is one of the imprints of Les Presses de l'Université d'Ottawa / University of Ottawa Press (PUO-UOP).

Other Literary Titles Published by the University of Ottawa Press

Literary Works

Denis Bachand, *L'énigme du carnet rouge*, 2026.
Marie-Claude Thifault (ed.), *La vie : c'est comme une bicyclette, il faut avancer pour ne pas perdre l'équilibre*, foreword by Florence Khoriaty, 2026.
Tareyn Johnson, *Dawaa: The Space in Between*, 2026.
Abla Farhoud, *Happiness Has a Slippery Tail*, translated from the French by Judith Weisz Woodsworth, 2025.
Jean-Louis Grosmaire, *Mouvance et espérance*, 2025.
Yolande Bastarache, *Détresse et nostalgie*, 2024.
Robert Major, *Éloge de la procrastination et autres facéties*, 2022.
Michel Picard, Kilis, 2021.
Jean-Louis Grosmaire, *Acadissima*, 2021. Prix France-Acadie.
Yolande Bastarache, *Mon village, la côte*, 2021.
Maurice Henrie, *Odette*, 2020.
Michel Picard, *Memoriam*, 2020.
Camilla Grudova, *L'alphabet des poupées*, translated from the English by Véronique Lessard and Marc Charron, 2020.
Maurice Henrie, *La maison aux lilas*, 2019.
Andrew F. Sullivan, *Tout vient à mourir*, translated from the English by Marc-André Clément, 2017.

Literary Non-fiction

Thomas Burelli, Alexandre Lillo, Lauren Touchant, Lynda Hubert Ta, and Elie Klee, *30 Climate COPs Later: Stories from Canadian Participants*, 2025.
Pierre Calvé, *Le français grandeur nature : portrait et défense d'une langue vivante*, 2025.
Nicole V. Champeau, *Pointe Maligne, retrouvée par les textes : présence française dans le Haut Saint-Laurent* (tome II), 2023.

Robert Major, *Identité, appartenances : un parcours franco-ontarien*, 2023.

Maurice Henrie, *La tête haute*, 2022. Prix du livre d'Ottawa.

Denis Bachand, *Voyages en nostalgie : parcours mémoriel à travers les arts et les médias*, 2021.

Robert Major, *Témiscamingue : châtiments, miracles, et autres propos du concierge de l'évêché*, 2021.

Robert Major, *Carnets du rang 5 : fragments d'un enracinement,* fragments d'un parcours, 2021.

Robert Major, *Mes conversations avec Claude*, 2019.

Biographies and Memoirs

Paul-François Sylvestre, *Lys, trillium et arc-en-ciel : doublement minoritaire,* 2025.

John Symon and Stéphane Desjardins, *Bob Silverman: The Impossible Hero / Bob Silverman : vélorutionnaire*, 2025.

Monique Aubry-Frize, *Une femme en ingénierie : mémoires d'une pionnière*, translated from the English by Suzanne Aubry, 2024.

Roy MacGregor, *L'étoile du nord : le mystère éternel de Tom Thomson et de la femme qui l'aimait*, translated from the English by Benoit Léger, 2023.

Fred Langan, *Elle a osé réussir : biographie de l'honorable Marie-P. Charette-Poulin / She Dared to Succeed: A Biography of the Honourable Marie-P. Charette*-Poulin, 2023.

Michel Bastarache and Antoine Trépanier, *What I Wish I Had Told My Children*, translated from the French by Julie Da Silva, 2023.

Stéphane Desjardins, *La famille Fermanian : l'histoire du cinéma Pine de Sainte-Adèle*, 2022.

Michel Bastarache and Antoine Trépanier, *Michel Bastarache : ce que je voudrais dire à mes enfants*, 2019.